Ro 10/13

2 5 OCT 2013

F

J
b
l
h
f
a
f
A
a
M
c
a
b
w

Leeds Library and Information Service
24 hour renewals
http://www.leeds.gov.uk/librarycatalogue
or phone 0845 1207271
Overdue charges may apply

Also by John Siddique

Recital

AN ALMANAC

JOHN SIDDIQUE

CAMBRIDGE

PUBLISHED BY SALT PUBLISHING
14a High Street, Fulbourn, Cambridge CB21 5DH United Kingdom

© John Siddique 2009

The right of John Siddique to be identified as the
author of this work has been asserted by him in accordance
with Section 77 of the Copyright, Designs and Patents Act 1988.

Salt Publishing 2009

Printed and bound in the United Kingdom by Biddles Ltd, King's Lynn, Norfolk

Typeset in Swift 9.5 / 13

ISBN 978 1 84471 514 5 hardback
ISBN 978 1 84471 723 1 paperback

Salt Publishing Ltd gratefully acknowledges
the financial assistance of Arts Council England

1 3 5 7 9 8 6 4 2

For my beloveds

Contents

Acknowledgements

With thanks to Sharon Olds for help with the poem 'Migratory Patterns,' and Mimi Khalvati for help with 'Other People's Children.' Thanks to Cherry Smyth and Catherine Smith for being my close readers. Poems from this book have appeared in the following publications:

ANTHOLOGIES

'Inside#1', 'Inside#2': *New Writing* 15 (British Council/Granta); 'Other People's Children': *Not in so many words* (Smith/Doorstop); 'Summer Cycle # 2', 'Summer Cycle # 3', 'Tree of the world', 'David': *Pendulum: a book of dreams* (Avalanche Books); 'Tree of The World': *Transparency* (Crocus); 'If You Want To Find Me': *Love Poems* (Suitcase Books).

MAGAZINES

'Unintended Loyalty': *London Magazine*; 'If You Want To Find Me': *Magma*; 'Summer Cycle #2': *Nthposition*; 'Summer Cycle #3 (Earth)': *Poetry Salzburg*; 'David': *Poetry Salzburg*; 'The Attic': *Poetry Salzburg*; 'Summer Cycle #5 (Cold Water)': *The Rialto*; 'Elegy — BRAND' Greenwich University; 'Facing You': *Journal of Pakistani Literature* (Vol 12.1).

Special thanks to: Abha Gautam, Xanthe Gresham, Stephen Hughes, John Holland, Rachel Mellor, Hannah Nunn, Euan & Ffion, Rose Howarth, Catherine Smith, Cherry Smyth, Kharumm Siddiqui, Marina Benjamin & Greg Klerkx, Erik & Birgit Peeters, this book is dedicated to each of these people.

Recital: *an almanac*

'The hardest thing in this world is to live in it,
be brave, live.'
>   —JOSS WHEDON : Buffy The Vampire Slayer 'The Gift'

'Everything that is made beautiful and fair and lovely
is made for the eye of one who sees.'
>   — RUMI

'You've got to get in to get out'
>   — GENESIS : *The Lamb Lies Down on Broadway*

Begin

and so this is a beginning (I seem
to know no other way, except the again and again)
racked up on top of every other beginning
all the way back to conception.

The again and again, a movement away
from confidence in the certainties,
to a confidence in beginning again
in the unknowing fog of the day which presents
itself, racking itself on top of every other day.
I use my fingertips feeling into it,
I have done this before and am confident
that the only thing I know
is that it is as different as the last.

You've Got to Get in to Get Out

The world will impinge into your need
for silence, into your prayers. In the hardest seconds
of your life, your neighbours will be drunk,
booming hip-hop through thin inconvenient walls.

At the lighting of your candles, in the moment
you need to focus — the apex of your flame,
the voice of the Holy Spirit, someone
will be vacuuming, talking, ringing up change,
a bin wagon bleeping as it reverses, builders
swearing into the distance you put by pulling into
yourself. It sounds like they are calling your name.

Birch Moon

Something to do with January,
something to do with after New Year.
Something to do with trying to make plans
for the year that never turn out,
but having to make them anyway.

Bootstrapping back to existence after
the duties of sonhood, husbandhood.
The hands moving faster on every clock,
especially the little one in the corner
of the computer screen.

Something names itself and gives meaning
under the duvet of last year's expectation.
Fifteen togs of keeping your eye on the ball.
Gas fires of ideas writing themselves.

One New Year's Eve

I drove two hours alone to the sea.
Stood on the beach at midnight, screaming
in the rush, while the fireworks
went off in the Welsh towns nearby.

Drove home slow, left the radio off.
Not wanting to arrive, the heater matrix
barely working, damn that old Volkswagen,
a fleece blanket over my freezing knees.

No one else out until I get to the city,
I'm so glad to go home alone tonight.

Facing You

We cannot tame the wind or the sea. Cannot
make them roll or blow our way. Taming ourselves
comes first, then we may laugh at them, scream at them.

We cannot tame those we wish to love. Cannot
make them roll or blow our way, but we can laugh
with them, scream with them, or break them in the taming
we try, which should be the fixing of ourselves.

We cannot tame love, or the wind, or the sea, we are not
here for long enough. There will always be these things.
Our joy comes from being the flash, the spark in the eye
of forever. Forever is grown too old to laugh and scream.

If You Want to Find Me

I'm the little boy again
building sanctuaries under beds,
staying in his room.

I have left the door on the latch.
Knock on the door, turn the handle.

It's not safe knowing your secrets.
You believe in the day,
I believe in the night.

I have left the door open,
I look busy but I'm waiting,
all full of flowers.
The daffodils of spring,
the roses of summer,
I'm green all winter.

The Other

He crashed into my life, everything I don't believe in,
took love away in a single action, so that even after years
it is fresh — the exact moment entwining my core.
It doesn't matter if I'm doing business,
or in the arms of my new wife, he is always with me.

Since that day I have had to beat my own heart.
Each day I have to spend time finding a reason to live,
the simplest things are heavier than they used to be.
I would like nothing more than to see a space
where he used to walk, nothing more than to strike
him and anyone who is like him from these pages.

It would be the easiest thing to make a war,
I could take my fury, my hurt and my truth.
No right thinking person would disagree with me.
I and all the right thinking people will be wrong
as we imprint our versions of the same horrors
into other lives. Once I swore a vow to god,
before that dust filled day when I cursed god
right back in the face. My vow was that this world
would be better for my living in it.
Now that god is gone I still believe the words.
One day I will remake something holy
from the piles of words we have stored up in defence.

Peace will not happen from war. My hurt is not your hurt.
If I do not choose peace, the terrorist in my dreams is given life,
so I spell forgiveness, learn it is not the same as forgetting,
learn that it means I have to stay away from him.
When the anger rises I have to go away and be quiet
or weep, or squeeze my fists. He has left me with a task
that makes me sick to my bones every single moment.
It is all I can do, no one notices, and this is my war.

Labyrinth

There is a ladder
in one of the walkways.
I occasionally
find my way into
a certain section
of the maze. I have
come to believe it is
the centre.

Here too you can see
a line of spheres on
the wall tops. I found
purchase beneath one
of them, managed to
climb up and push it,

it did not move.
It was heavy like
concrete, but had no
temperature to gauge,
like the walls, they
have mass but neither
heat nor cold.

I have come to call
a region home. By making
marks I have mapped and
understood the layout.

I am not sure of the purpose
of the structure.
There are many stories.
The drive to go beyond

this section is overwhelming.
To find a way onto the wall,
see it spread out and to
choose a clear direction.

Rowan Moon

Some days are over before they begin.
Sleeping past the alarm, eating cornflakes
standing in the kitchen. Looking at the viewless view,
the next row of houses, Hannah and her cats
and children, Graham filling his water bottle.

How do you pull a sickie when you work for yourself?
You'd be paranoid about running into yourself all day.
So it's out to the car, making the miles, marking the time.
A sandwich for lunch. The long drag through the afternoon.

Some days begin where you least expect them to.
A girl on a checkout pauses the conveyer belt for a moment,
says something about the DVD you're buying,
how much the film meant to her. You tell her your little story
and the day begins for both of you.

February Verses

Light returns and ice bakes itself
onto cars. Tentative beginnings
when I had lost belief in newness.

The inner journey is no escape,
neither is the outward bound.
Birds swoop and flock at evening.

Tree branches — ungloved fingers
against a sky of white paint.
I had come to believe that nothing existed

beyond the sense that something must.
A dash of colour through white paint,
a friend telling a stranger my name.

Unintended Loyalty

On a night in nineteen sixty-nine
my mother and father are asleep.
They have put their holy war
on to their nightstands, Islam on one table,
Catholicism across the room on the other.

They sleep with the bodily intention
of keeping distance, faces pushed
into sleep like they're pressed against glass,
his penis limp on his thigh, her openness pulled
between her legs with the curving of her back.

The night moves them so that her black hair
curls on to his shoulder. Coils of bed-springs
roll them towards the centre of the bed.
His brown arm moves over her white side.
When they wake they will dress again,
taking nothing of each other into the day.

Ash Moon

Venus in the morning sky, the Ash Moon,
a chopping blade moving closer to earth.
Her gravity lifting yellow crocus heads
to attention, moving cold sap through veins.

The ideas I've held onto for nearly ten years
seem thin in the clear light. Jupiter increases,
his storms are old, my storms are old.
There is no new again. There is now and however.

Your cards reply to my letter, it is time
to finish things. Time to stop trying
to impose order. Saturn is east of the Sun.

I cut the cards into four, light them in a candle flame.
Mix sage with the ash for cleanliness, for clarity.
Not burning your names, but releasing the lives
we've imposed order on. The salsa band plays,
no one is dancing, the band haven't got anything else.

I hang red ribbon strips on the door posts.
Coins wrapped in red paper, given to the kids
for prosperity. Smoke releasing us to new paths.
White sage making imposition a choice.
The wind tossed Moon cuts up the stars.
Sagittarius is running ahead of the morning.

Recital

I'd like to give you a temporary
name until you are old enough to know
yourself. Then one day you will tell me who
you are in one of the conversations we have,
where we start out funny and go to sad,
then serious, then back to funny again.

If we were allowed to wait to say who
we are, giving ourselves names as if putting
the words to rising music, that is scored
from continuance and newness, not to name
you after me or my mother, or your mother's mother,

but unmaking the concretized image of family,
you might put yourself together from the combinations
you see in your growing, or you may never name that song,
or find the words to complete the recital of yourself.

David

It's fourteen years since that New York spring,
when we arrived in full snow. Travelled north
to retreat, made sheet ice sculptures on the lake
with the view of the atomic power station.

Just as the thaw melts the white world, we're driving,
invited to stay in the city of towers.
A small sliver of a flat in Greenwich Village,
all night coffee crowds, real live porn on tv.

From up the Empire State you can see everything.
From the World Trade Centre you can see even more.
Below us the building is half empty, scrappy offices,
rooms too numerous to fill.

We were eagles casting shadows with our hands
on the harbour, dream-catchers on this observation platform.
Bridges span the brown river. We were great friends then,
trying to photograph 360 degrees, friends with shared beliefs.

Trying to start ahead of ourselves. Making statements
and precepts to right the world instead of being ourselves.
There was no parting, or angry words. Our foundations
were built on speeches. Some friendships are like family,
ours was a series of agreements.
We agreed for a decade, then one day we didn't.

Red Line (He Loves Me)

There is a red line extending through
a past from my heart all the way back through
a series of cut out paper shapes,
images of my father, his large presence
when I am a small boy, the gaps in between
his returns after my parents' split,
the moments of each of his reappearances.

The red line has been covered in leaves,
covered in footprints, forgotten from the map.
I have driven other roads, taken different trains,
eavesdropping conversations, holding on
to love so tightly in the absence of the line.

It lay untraced for thirty years, there but unseen,
present but not spoken about, walkable
in the space of heartbeats once rediscovered.

His large presence when I am a small boy.
The man of now wanting his father's love.
The gaps between his returns, when I am full
of other stories so that I don't need him.
The moments between each returning,
when in his losing his grip on his family
he tried over and again to demonstrate his love.

There is a red line extending from
my father's heart to my heart. I have swept
the leaves and cleared the dirt from it.
The grown man can love his loves, kiss rather
than fear loss, pull tension into the bow of love,
launching arrows tied with red streamers
into the very sky

Alder Moon

The spring fair arrives with its doughnuts
and goldfish. — Electro pop instead of Calliopes.

The fire has returned to the Northland.
The sun and moon balance on either hand.

We try going without coats, beginning
to talk again after wintering, anointing ourselves

with tea. Making plans and sewing seeds
to reap in the late summer.

There are jobs to do. — T-shirts to wear,
the frost might still have some surprises.

The light wakes the dawn at a decent hour.
Venus disappears in the morning twilight.

Changing clothes and changing hair,
the year begins, we're caught a little short,

three months behind, with the sun in our faces,
we look towards. The moon moving her fingers

in the backs of our heads. Orion keeps his sword
sheathed, watching our wheels.

Elegy

Mirror, shave — loose cheeks.
A handful of water for each year.
Bristle harder, more silver.
Scything Gillette — hot water.

Tea standing in the kitchen.
Light above the roofs.
Last star, leftover moon,
leaves hang with the cold,
counting out internal time.

Steam plumes from boiler outlet.
What is next? I
don't want to wake you.
Lean into fridge hum,
watch for the post to come.

Willow Moon

The moon is unaffected by April's storms.
A wedding ring is taken off and lost.

We should have worn our coats, it is cold
on the shaded side of the street.

We should have worn our coats, it is not
as warm as we thought it was going to be.

The willow twists, bends in the April storms.
Oak and pine break and are lost.

A withy of willow thrown down by the rain,
I'll put it as a garland around my head.

We should have worn our coats.
Willow drains water from the ground.

We should have worn our coats, wanting
it to be later on than it is. I should have worn

my coat, pinned a sprig on my lapel to quietly
tell of your leaving for the greenwood.

Silence

My father with a three-week beard hiding his mouth.
A pocket with a torn lining.

When you think your train is moving out of the station,
but it's the train at the next platform stirring itself.

The well made corners of my parents bed.

What you were going to say before you asked the question.
The white inside of an eggshell.

Before you and after you.

The surprise of a razor cut in the morning.

Your hand supporting your questions.

A small wetness of spittle at the corner of your mouth.
A chalked equals sign on a blackboard.
My head in your lap.

Between the water and the reflection.
Looking above the facades.
Fingernail shine, arm hair, brow space.

Migratory Patterns

His arrival into town caused few heads to turn,
he is always the stranger, along with the other strangers,
he flows using projected blankets of ideas to keep himself.

His fanfare is one of factory hooters. Red trumpets set high,
calling the workers in. Dandelion clocks let
themselves go into the breeze defying industrialisation,
the tarmac, the routines of migrants.

At Dexine's Rubber Compounds he's carrying
hot, freshly moulded blanks from machine to machine,
my father shows me how to hold my voice in.
His clean brow, his steady mouth,
intercontinental in his white shirtsleeves.

At night, in sleep, his body would let him go back,
dandelion seeds caught in his uprising desire,
until half way between my fifth and sixth years
he pulled back from being a migrant.
He left me a look I sometimes see when I'm shaving,
pushing my cheek towards the magnifying mirror,
looking close for the next stroke, our eyes are the same.

Because he is gone he is present. Because he is young
in my mind, he is still young. He kept on moving,
back to the east in sleep, so many nights, he had to go home.

Hawthorne Moon

Summer is finally here, we say,
or,
isn't it cold? Summer's a month behind,
or,
last year was so much hotter,
or
when the hell will it begin?
And,
the circle we live is a triangle,
we have lived it life after life.

Aquarius is invisible in the morning sun
just over the southern horizon.

Light gets caught sometimes in a prism,
it goes in but doesn't come back out,
total internal reflection.

Triangle or circle it doesn't stop us shining
our lights life after life.
Or, isn't it time,
we found the gap in the circumference?
Or,
isn't it time we loved ourselves inside and out?
Or,
when will we?

Keeping On

Here is the morning, here are the cats on the bed.
Here is the Pennine rain, here are the papers full
of people who know nothing about you or me,
telling me repeatedly 'it's time, it's time.'

It's a safer world they say, but I'm afraid of the street,
afraid of my neighbours, everyday I fill myself in.

I'll get out of bed, breathe in and out.
Yes it's a conscious effort, to breathe,

and I'm going to breathe. I'm going to walk
these roads, I'm going to talk to strangers,
and smile at your children, I'm going to ask
for a cup of tea when all my mates
say let's get lashed. I'm going make words
fit the pictures, I'm going to take time to find out,
walk out of step with your step, say I don't know,
step into my own shadow, eat my greens.

Oak Moon

It would seem that it is night, a sulphurous moon
in a sky painted by a child casts long shadows
of houses and you and I. You've worn your green dress,
I'm entirely naked on the driveway of our house.
You hold your hands in your unmade lap, head tilted
in comment. I have a smile, imperfect in body,
I just want to walk here. Instead of telling me
to *get back inside*, you say that you love me,
let them look and pass. Some days will do this,
make you need to be naked outside your own house.
You are beautiful in your green dress
with your hands in a bunch, holding me up.

Trade

All summer, huge ox-eyed daises, their petals
a circle of moon white moth wings, opening
to the light. Closing to the dusk and the evening.

All summer my brown eyes drinking in
interconnection, the wheels of god.

The daisies, pure sex, moving with the hours.
Just daisies; loving the day, spooning up to it.

Playing in the long hours, up to my knees in them.
Just a boy, loving the day. Spooning a 12 year-old's
simples into my throat, before sex became a politic,
a trade-off, a key.

Inside

1 'IT IS NO USE SHOUTING'

There are poems to write which I am told should
not be written, almost as if to think
about a thing condones it. We are supposed
to say this is bad, this is good, this is evil.

I am part of it. We have the minds that could
make these things, but what interests me is the way
you hold your hand to your face at that moment,
the film of sweat above your lip. There is
an answer there.

2 'There is no more time'

9.47, the peak of the morning rush is
beginning to subside, though the tube is
closed so he's taking the bus to work.
A woman at the front of the bus is
on her way to her course. There is
a girl on her way to the dentist, and
a cleaner on her way home. A bus full
of people like this and more.

Then there is no more time, just a flash.
No time for fear. Here then gone, or
unconscious, or at the edge, or screaming.
All fixed in their own heads a moment ago,
busy being late for things, tired, looking forward
to a cup of tea, or just getting there
to get out of this traffic.

9.47 lasts forever and ticks on for the rest of us.
Before and after the application of words. Divide
the hour, divide the minute, sub-divide the second,
keep on dividing and time ceases to exist.

3 'THIS IS WHAT YOU WERE BORN FOR'

How do you pull that far inside? Far enough
to forget the people around you, or
perhaps you can feel their every thought and
movement as they talk, stare into the middle
distance, think about things they shouldn't,
fiddling with their phone buttons.
Preparing, pulling inside, a prayer
for all that's left behind. 'God give me
the strength to do this at the required time.
God is greater. God is Greater. Let this blood
be the fuse.' Inside, pulling inside.
Make the contact. Pulling inside.

4 'Nobody knows why'

Walk past the Costcutter supermarket
open 24 hours, a withered shrine of tape,
paper, poems and flowers, a football shirt,
a bottle of beer for Jean Charles de Menezes.

Stockwell station has no ceiling tiles,
tangled metal rods, cold lights, speakers,
wire and air ducts all exposed.

Through the ticket barrier, then the escalator,
'Blue is the new pink.'
'See the coolest show in town this summer.'
Airline adverts, and a bold yellow lion face
for The Lion King.

The stairs with their use polished edge protectors,
almost golden, nickel cut diamond squares,
jewellery for the passageways. Grey tiles, bare wall.
The posters say, *Stockwell is undergoing
a major refurbishment. Station Improvements.*
There are also posters appealing for witnesses
for the Independent Police Commission investigation
into the shooting of Jean Charles de Menezes.

There are no shrines on the platform, it looks like
any tube station. Run and jump onto the standing train.
The white flash of violence and ending.
The soul's inability to have time for the shock to register.
The shots still ring out here without any outward sign.

Holly Moon — Scalpsie Bay

The sea turns everything to bone.
I can see my own skeleton
in the driftwood, the city mind
wants to see the end, or find
some meaning in the runic arrangements,
the sea turns everything to bone.

My cities where I would contemplate
loneliness amongst the lonely, are gone.
There is no thought outside of the rhythm,
The crunch of shingle, the background of the sea.

You have to love what you love.
Showing me what I already know,
what I refuse to take in. Each thing
has its bones, it goes on, known,
forgotten, washed white as stone.

Accumulations

Now it has stopped raining, the street reconvenes its dailies.

Now it has stopped raining, chive heads no longer have the will
to come back up. There has been no rhythm to the rains.

I want to sit inside the rain, be sheathed by it.
Looking up, the last drips are zip-lines from trees
each one seems it will break the pavement.

These last drops are wetter than the rain itself, as if
the moisture has been saving itself to surprise me.

Now that the street has reconvened. Now that it has stopped raining.
Now that there is no rhythm. Now that the sheath has lifted.

Summer Cycle

1 THE LIST

Is there a list of wives or husbands
written up for us somewhere before we're born?

You meet one of them every now and then,
and both of you know it, it goes beyond

recognition into innate knowledge. You could
talk and pick up a story from years ago,

yet you have never even spoken until now,
should you say something in this moment.

You know each other and always have.
You are happily married, or she is, or

both of you are, or are not. Meeting once,
this time, quite by accident, then forming part

of the continuum of the rest of your lives,
though it is always in absence and possibility.

2 Waking in the Night

I wake in the television static of 3.40.
A voice on the phone, then it's gone,
she'd misdialed an old number.

I'd forgotten the sound of her voice.
I think about my family back home
and I let her sound play through me.
She's in a new world; new friends, a new husband.
I'm a new beginning, though something keeps me
moving from place to place with work.

In vague and familiar rooms, we'll
take up new lives, while the spider's web
of inferences spun in the night hangs
jewelled with moisture under the windowsill,
connecting wood and stone with its threads.
Almost translucent. Strong and ready.

3 EARTH

I tread lightly because the earth is broken.
Lightly not out of choice, my legs won't reach
the ground. Fear of breaking it further
congeals in my quadriceps. I want to walk
on the ground, am sick of being air.

I tread lightly. The earth is full of memory.
To stand squarely on the ground is
to remember. It remakes the circuit,
the slamming static build-up will ground itself
in one blue arc. It stops the heart.

The electrical jolt fires the most important
of muscles. Nerves burn like a fuse box
in an old house. The box in the cellar
where we put away our clutter, where I
find ideas of ourselves after you've gone.

I tread lightly. I walk past where we used
to live. That part of town has closed its doors.
The earth's arms ready to take me when I fall
to her. The earth's weight ready to take
the best and the worst of us. The earth does not
forsake what was and what is. I tread lightly

throwing down salt to bleach the pavement.
Placing soil on the breast of the dead. Kicking
at the four posts that form the directions
to try to bring the sky down.

I tread lightly. Each step down begins
a journey they say. Each step down begins
a time-line. I see future histories
radiate from each step of connection,
they fly out in blue sparks; wishes, promises,
and time-lines. I would rather not know where
these paths lead. To just follow one like a tram line;
two rails and their sleepers, always the same
distance apart as they perspective to an horizon.

I flail my legs like a boy with too many balloons,
or a big golf umbrella caught in the wind. Reach
for the earth and repel from the earth. The earth
won't forget or let me sleep until I give her my weight.

4 Creation myth

There was a forest of only one tree. Her shadow
changing length as it clocks her presence. One tree
growing into her tasks; to be a tree, a forest,
a nest, to clean the air, photosynthesis, be green.

When the birds come, it is almost too much. Every bird
in the world nesting in the one tree that is a forest. Every bird
using her twigs, eating her seed. To hold your arms out
forever, taking the nesting weight every day.

At the edge of the forest is a poppy. A single flower
trying to be a field. Her names are success and oblivion.
Burning in her poppiness, in her short summer.
At night she breathes her redness up to the face of the moon.

The sun falls in love with the forest. The summer blows away
with the petals and leaves. The newlyweds autumn
and winter together. A difficult year for them both to marry,
he is often away, but he's not going anywhere. He always
comes home from his business. The forest is always a forest,
a sundial for him, he makes her shadow.
She is his proof of life, his landmark.

This year a field of poppies, an acre of success and oblivion,
waiting for each summer to fill all summers.

5 Cold water

Washing faces and forearms in the river.
Washing our feet, calves, the bodily heat.
Washing out the snot from our noses.
Cleaning the root of the tongue.

Tearing dog roses full of redness.
Handfuls of petals on the surface.
Letting words go with the flower heads,
letting the words cleanse the root of

the tongue. River of words, undulating
heavy mirror. The magnetic coldness,
stones slippery with angel hair weed
dancing along down in the cold.

Hazel Moon

I am the salmon in the pool
I am the estuary leaving the river
I am nine hazels gathered from the ground
I am your own force turned back on yourself
I am the poem that must be written
I am the fire of the earth
I am the earth on fire
I am a moonless night
I am a secret held on paper
I am the housemartin at dawn
I am the first spot of rain
I am water for your harvest
I am a rider on horseback
—distant thunder

Without

I became a five-pointed star
high at the edge of the atmosphere,
the edge of space. Australia is coming
into view. The oceans turn.

Down there is my house. Down there
is my body, if I opened my eyes could
I see this star? Just one more night-light,
or a fast-moving satellite.

A cord keeps us navel-to-navel,
if it were to break now I'd move beyond
the known. I am not frightened,

the whole of time would only seem
like a moment. How far will I fall
in that minute? I want to move so
deep I am home again.

Involution

There is a town north of here where I'm told
the people are all survivors of small intimate
personal disasters. A whole town of people
who for whatever reasons have all been left
behind. I went there for a while to see if
it was true, all I could tell was that no one
looked like they had had sex in a long while,
not good sex that is, that glues you back together.
But they do couple and uncouple at a furious
rate, no relationship gets past five years,
and there are so many children born of these
couplings who won't leave when they're grown.

Promises

My wrists are burnt and bleeding,
Chinese burns, rope burns, pressure marks.
I do the same for you with each of these words,
each word a knot of ego or identity to be undone,
using our bodies to go where there are no words,
as we play shibari without safety,

each promise a loss of the sensual,
we try to hold together bind our lives into
what we'd like to be. Darling, we change ourselves
into each other's ideas, ceasing to be the fire,
the excitement we were for each other
in syllabic increments.

Tied up in red, in elegant silk,
in gorgeous language. Tied up trying. Tied up losing
our lives whilst making tourniquets of these ropes,
of need, desire and loneliness.

shibari: the Japanese art of bondage

Attersee

We are left with ourselves, endless footprints
of water, each one a small sky.

The sea goes further out than the inclination
to stand at its edge, so far out to become
a purple mirage.

Looking up to a storm crossing the distance,
it won't come here, we are safe enough.

Close our eyes—ceasing to talk, it turns
through us both. I would say something to you
if I could, I would kiss you if I could.
I touch your face as though I may break.

Vine Moon — Fire

I will not lie in the earth,
I will be consumed in flame.

I will not ask for forgiveness,
from my mother or family.

I learned from each thing,
I loved from each thing.

When I was wrong,
I was wrong.

Words of punishment and eternity
mean nothing in these seconds.

I will enter the fire
as a man who has taken
the perfect lover for his body,
the smell of her sex still on me.

A white-hot pyre, or a flaming raft,
better by fire than the endless earth.

Beachcombing

Old music from the sea, a flugelhorn
washed up on Dungeness' shore of polished stones.
The copper turned to green, the horn bust, buckled,
the valves rusted permanently into place,
no more playing fingers moving their mechanisms
in their oiled wards. No mouthpiece, no kiss
of a musician's breath passing through the tubes.
It's a heavy carcass I drag up the beach,
twelve or fifteen pounds of awkward shaped metal
that once played Bach or parped alone in practice.
Music thrown overboard in some uprising
or mutiny off the Dorset coast,
hung on my garden wall against tar black,
open to the sea air, mute in its orchestration.

Standing There and Here

Floor to ceiling and wall to wall.
A single ended fish tank. The wet edge
of a pool. Sixteen floors up. An expanse
of curtain pulled back. I see the storms roll in
from Preston, making their way across the lands
of Lancashire. Clouds are white emulsion in water.

From this balcony the urge to leap
and fall. Dave downstairs plays his AC/DC loud.
Kat next door is doing the dishes, the cups chinking
on the drainer. Knoll hill, the kneecap of the horizon,
always my focal point, my hill beacon.
I see the fire that isn't there.

A Change

I feel your menopause in my body.
Feel the slowing, the stopping, the fear.

And the time of children is ending,
just a few more years.
The iron of menstrual blood
electrifies. I hate the smell,

but I'll miss it. Our one catch at parenthood lost.
You were bleeding too heavily,
you blame your age. I tried every way to hold you,
to tell you it was alright, that we would live for the child.

And we bound each other with promises.
Made each other's reflections with promises.

And we draw new life for ourselves from our bodies,
amid the slowing, the fear and the stopping,
and sometimes I wonder at his name.

Ivy Moon

At the end there were only words.
The words survived our flesh.

Then you said let it be dark,
and it was dark,

and I said as long as there
are words we go on.

There is no separating out.
Speak in to the dark and it is good,

and we made a firm promise of
those words, there will be no division.

We took back the day and night.
Undid our concepts of heaven and hell.

Spun the day and the night back
into the clock.

Let us be dark, without image.
No longer trying to see what is good.

The Attic

It took until the October after your divorce,
then we climbed into the attic, where the infrequent
parts of your marriage had been put away
with the girl you used to be.—The girl who shaved
her teddy's belly when he needed an operation.

Dancing around each other cooking bacon and pasta,
while you bodily process what comes and what goes,
the infrequent things that make a marriage.
We cook together, it is almost our favourite sport.
Then we get the black bin bags ready for Oxfam.

My Father

Where in the world are you? Did you go home?
or are you dead? I feel you in me
but that could just be an idea in my chest.

You are an 8mm film, but you're never in it.
You're holding the camera, those are my fat
little legs. Without sound we are funny animations.
We live through the lens in vivid colours.

Watching; tiny film runs through projector sprockets,
brought back by a lamp and a lens. Those are my fingers
making silhouette dogs; biting my onscreen hand.
I could almost turn around quickly and see you
leaning over the reels. You've been quiet
all evening showing me myself. I have no voice
for you. Twelve feet of single frames playing for
two and a half minutes.

Autumn Tree

A white wind and a leafless tree, larch branch
against larch wind. Last year's leaves make soft ground
under this year's shedding. A leafless tree
in a white wind. Larch peeling away from itself.

Yew Moon

The first life passed like a dream and then smoke.
The second life was all about you.
The third life begins, we are Russian dolls
to ourselves, sloughing off our larger versions,
becoming more contained, and capable
of containing less. Each life that goes feels
like an end, until the new doll learns to be animate.
Never knowing when or if we have reached
the smallest doll, after which there are no others,
a solid seed of ourselves. Then only theories, religious
arguments and scientific blankness. A million books
try to define the root of what comes next
in this sequence of painted wood.

Bonfire Night

Every year around bonfire night, when the town is swarming,
the posters go up of the murdered schoolgirl Lindsay Rimer.
She went to the off licence and didn't come home again.
She is every thirteen-year-old girl you've ever seen waiting
for a school bus, her skirt a little too short on purpose
for her coltish thighs, pink in the November evening air.
Her flirting legs and her big heeled Clarks' shoes, worn at the edge
where she awkwardly tilts her foot when she's talking to boys.
Her brown hair the same length as my daughter's, who is ten,
but will wear her skirt too short and her heels too high
in a few year's time. The poster asks if anyone knows anything,
to please come forward. Ten years hold their tongue.
She should've had her heart broken by now, travelled to India,
made some serious mistakes. The canal knows. It is very cold
at this time of year running over its aqueduct just before the park,
where the annual firework display shivers the smoked air.

Filofax

The ordinary things come round again,
like full moons and filofax refills,
bank holidays and the not so far off
Epiphany of January.

This day reminds you of a sister.
This day reminds you to remember.
A week across two pages.

Ordinary things come round again,
like ordering stationery & the feeling you get
realising New Year's Eve will be here again.

Marking days across two pages.
What if someone who didn't know you,
were to take these notes and write a story?
Your small fine writing in black gel pen,
the possibility of a phone number
in the unlined blank space, a whole week blocked out
with a single word, 'Vienna'.

To read the book of this year—Advent Sunday,
Thanksgiving (USA,) Week 47.

Wintering Geraniums

Nobody has given me any news
of you in a long time. You're becoming
a person in a photo album without
a name next to them. As much as I want
to pick up a pen and write it in, I don't.

You are forming into someone new.
The vividness is fading. Next year's flowers
will look the same as this years. They have
the same root, but have different petals.

Elder Moon

A butterfly, a red admiral, wakes
me flitting its wings against the lampshade.
It's December, it's cold out there. Not knowing
what to do, I let it into another room.

Last night's talk goes back into its box
as I catch the butterfly in a glass,
gently sliding paper underneath to preserve
its legs. Conversations wait for us as patiently
as street signs or bus stops, we could put our trust
in them to guide us, but we keep on taking
the same routes, walking the same paths, saying
the same things, having deja vus.

This morning the butterfly is in my room again,
fluttering against the window behind
the heavy curtains. The trees are bare,
the frost has a solid hold on the garden,
dimmed and nectarless.
I click the latch and it flies fast,
away from the heat and the house.

Annunciation of The Virgin

My mother changes her date of birth by a day
to share today with her Blessed Lady,
seven or eight years old telling everyone
that this is her birthday.

After church on Sunday, after school
—wearing her medal, the 'Holy Angels'
would meet for prayer group, a row of young girls
in the squat brown church on John Street. In a line
at the pews, the wide green ribbon and the large
embossed image of Mary joining her hands.

In nineteen forty-two, sirens destroy thought,
everyone's running, carrying their gas mask.
The ARP man yelling '*get moving*,'
driving the terrified through the routine
of air raid. British spitfires, darting housemartins,
going down to Belfast to protect
Samson and Goliath, the ship cranes at Harland & Woolf.

Her family are running, to get to the safety
of the country. In the war years no bombs
will fall on Portadown. My mother full
of streets and noise is dawdling—they could all be killed
today, half of the equation of my genes
lost with her chromosome map.

She gets left behind as the swarm moves.
Left under the tunnel bridge of grey iron,
coin sized rivets, railway vibrations.
Mary comes as my mother calls her mother to wait.
White robes, white veil, Mary bows her face down
close to Norah's, arms widening in a line
to stop her right there, then to guide her like a rail.

The 52nd Week of the Year
(for Richard Kinsey 14/12/47 to 24/12/07)

It is that week of the year,
when all our lives search for balance.
A single or a billion 'no mores'
resonating in mind. We've been home for days,
slept a lot, eaten a lot, made a bit more love,
or been wholly inappropriate.

Someone always dies at this time;
something about Christmas and New Year
sees them off. As I watch people with faces
similar to my dead neighbour load boxes
and bits into the backs of cars, I wonder
what I know, what maps are laid out
in my mind? What knowledge is there?
Lots of books and music, a few snippets
on human nature, and how to block out
a story for the telling. I think I know
some things about the people I love,
perhaps as I know my own face lightly reflected
in the window glass. Watching Richard's family
divide his world, boxes of books and CDs.
Who is looking after his dog?

Next year, I say, *will be about acting
from the things I know.* Tightrope walking,
praying for change when things restart,
praying for my neighbour's soul whilst watching
his outward shows be valued then separated
by quiet forceful voices into mine and yours.

To Reading

At this time of year I give thanks that it is
getting dark earlier, I like the days to have clear endings.

I stand and look at the spectrum of book spines,
waiting for something to take the bait. I should
get round to getting rid of this wallpaper
that has been here since before I moved in.
The dehumidifier in the cellar clicks back on,
drip by drip preserving us. With each sampling
of words I'm building bonfires, catching trains,
hearing other voices talking over my own,
until I am caught between the drips,
still standing, resting back against the wall.

Other People's Children

He is eight and good at football. His mind
flits blacker and whiter than a magpie
from Playstation to plastic sword, chocolate,
internet, to nothing to do, to slamming the ball.
He has a will of iron. Can bend his mother's
and my love for him like plasticine;
when he wears his stick-on tattoos
in the same place on his shoulders as I have mine,
when he calls me 'old chappy,' as we scream
through the air as human aeroplanes.
I want so much to show him the world
I know, make it right for him.
Their Dad shows up every now and then,
it blows this family sideways, the guy ropes
twang off their pegs, until morning comes
and the wind dies down, and he goes off again.
I begin planting and parenting. Applying constancy
at the thin end of myself. But here is the boy
on a Saturday morning, next to me in bed,
hugging his mother and I together,
blowing at my chest hair.

Tree of the World

On nights when the sounds of the children
we should have had wake me, I sit in the yellow
of the bulb, and place my hands upon the horizon,
spin on the axis mundi which connects us,

even though at times we have no desire to be connected.
The stones on the moor, touched by so many
over the centuries, will speak our confessions,
if we will just stand, lay our hands and listen at the centre.

The carvings of spirals and swastikas, concentric rings
and bloodlines, added to over millennia, will fade
in eternity's face. Each year a wipe of a cloth over rough stone.
Soon they'll be polished and faceless, then sand on the wind.

I will wait for you there, where the symbols
lose their meanings, where our attempts
at holding on are less than nothings, but still the axis,
nameless and unspeakable, is true, never out of sight.

The All I See is Your Face

The all I see is your face
as an afterlight when I close
my eyes, which lifts each moment
away from shadows, from legacies
of the past, stories I tell myself
of what should come next.

Framed by the main light
of your moment,
resorting to prayer to walk
the narrow way, I close my eyes
—trusting the after image
          —the all I see is your face.

With you I am in a corridor
of sun, darkness at its edges
as we walk around town looking up,
looking at sky and drinking tea.
In all other company
          —the all I see is your face.

The Death of Death

Whatever I write is incomplete, the words
are not enough of a thing, incomplete
in comparison and allusion.
The page and the thing itself are two poems.
A blue sky, a lively breast, a body of trees,
these things are themselves, ink and paper are not
even a facsimile. If the moment could
be written down, it would mean the end
of books, the plough would make the verse ready
for the seed, love could be permanent
so that forgetting would lose its power.

This I what I ask of each book,
it is why each writer fails. We can but try.
One day, one of us will find the way,
a notebook left with a line three quarters written,
we will become immortal as libraries of true moments,
then both god and death will be conquered.

Lightning Source UK Ltd.
Milton Keynes UK
UKOW04f0059130913

217085UK00002B/24/P